This pygmy owl has moved into a woodpecker's nest, safe inside a saguaro; this 50-foot tall cactus is a reservoir of water and has edible fruits.

Careful! The bandicoot grows up to 31 inches long, including its tail, and eats insects, worms, and sometimes very small mammals and lizards.

This desert toad has just emerged. It has been waiting nine months, buried in the sand like a mummy, for the rains to come.

Its huge ears give the fennec very sharp hearing. They also help cool its body.

To stay cooler, the chameleon of the Kalahari touches the ground with only two feet at a time.

For Nils, Marie-Esther, and Magnus

With thanks to Pierre Bertrand

First published in the United States of America in 2001
by Walker Publishing Company, Inc.
Published simultaneously in Canada by Fitzhenry and Whiteside,
Markham, Ontario L3R 4T8
Originally published in France in 1999 under the title *Vide, le désert?*

Library of Congress Cataloging-in-Publication Data
available upon request.
ISBN 0–8027–8765–7 (hardcover)
ISBN 0–8027–8766–5 (reinforced)

The artist used acrylic paint on paper to create the illustrations for this book.

Book design by Rosanne Kakos-Main

Printed in Hong Kong

10 9 8 7 6 5 4 3 2 1

DESERT TREK

An Eye-Opening Journey through the World's Driest Places

MARIE-ANGE LE ROCHAIS

Translated from the French by George L. Newman

Walker & Company
NEW YORK

The desert:

People often think of it as nothing more than a vast area of sand, an empty, lifeless wasteland burned by the sun, where thirst reigns supreme . . . but is the desert truly empty?

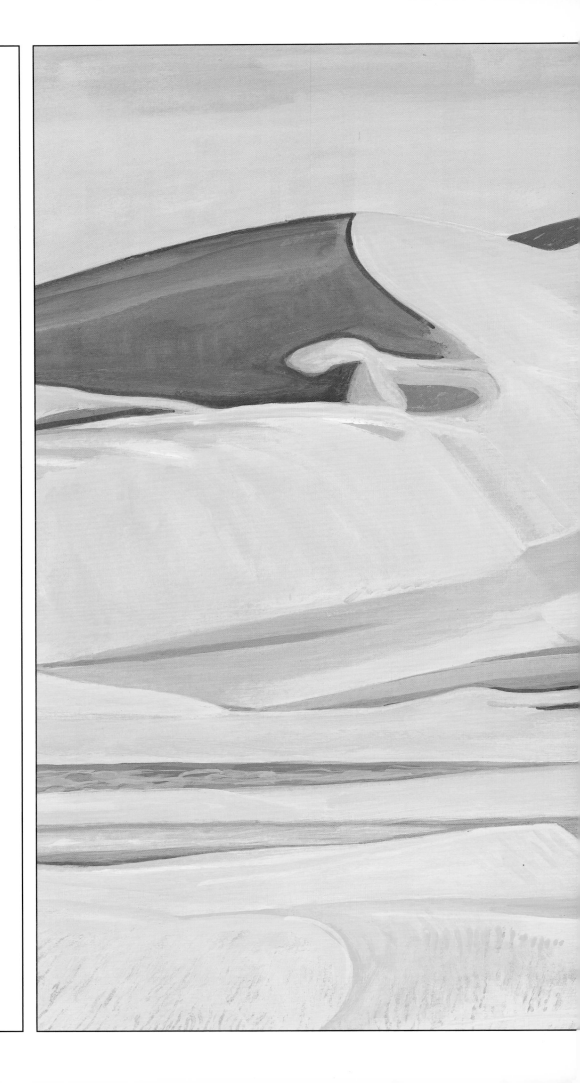

There are people in the desert.

In the Sahara live people called the Tuaregs, also known as the "blue people." The nickname comes from a type of blue cloth they wear. Tuareg raiders and traders of the past, who covered their faces with veils, earned the name "warriors of the blue veil." The covering protects the face from the sun and the wind-driven desert sand, and from evil spirits that the Tuaregs believe snatch at people's hair. Adult males wear a veil in the presence of women, strangers, and in-laws.

Traditionally, the Tuaregs are wandering nomads who raise cattle and camels. Crossing the desert with their caravans, they transport gold, ivory, salt, ebony, and spices. They know the invisible routes through the shifting sand that will lead them from watering hole to watering hole until they safely reach their destination.

There are oases in the desert.

The oasis is a fertile area that provides refuge in the arid desert. It is where the caravans and migrating birds stop to rest. People who live in the oasis look forward to the arrival of a caravan, because it brings merchandise and news from the world beyond the desert.

The oasis has a source from which people can draw water to irrigate their orchards and fields, creating paradises of green. Water has been trapped far below the sands of the Sahara for millions of years, dating from a time when the land was covered with forests, marshes, and lakes.

The date palm is the most valuable tree grown at the oasis, and the people make use of every part of it. They eat its fruit, the date, and the seeds are ground up and fed to livestock. Its wood is used for construction, its large leaves to cover roofs, and its sap to make a beverage.

There is irrigation in the desert.

In the Mojave Desert of the United States, modern technology helps people pump great amounts of water from underground to create swimming pools, green lawns, and golf courses.

All around the world, people use up vast amounts of freshwater to bring life to arid regions. The danger in doing this is that we consume reserves of water that were stored in the earth a very long time ago, when the climate of the region was wet. A similar problem affects the Aral Sea in central Asia. The major rivers that feed the sea have been diverted to irrigate fields of cotton. As a result, more than half of the Aral Sea has been dried up.

Unfortunately, there is not enough rain in the desert to replenish these reserves. What will happen when they run out?

There are plants and animals in the desert.

For millions of years, plants and animals have been able to survive with little water in the desert.

During the driest part of the year, some plants die, but their seeds can spend years in the soil, waiting for the right moment to germinate. With the first rain, the Mojave Desert becomes covered with multicolored, fragrant flowers. Plants like the saguaro cactus collect hundreds of gallons of water in their trunks when it rains.

Some desert plants are very useful to people. For example, jojoba produces an oil that is used in items like soap and shampoo. Plants such as mesquite and yucca are used to make medicines.

The animals that live in the desert get their water from the plants they eat or the flesh of their prey. They are able to go long periods without drinking. They also find shelter during the hottest part of the day to reduce the amount of water they need.

There are waves in the desert.

At the edge of some deserts, there is a large body of water. The Namib, a coastal desert in southwestern Africa, for example, is bordered by the Atlantic Ocean.

The Namib's waves of dunes give way to the waves of the sea. So many boats have wrecked on the treacherous offshore reefs that the coastline is littered with their rusted hulks. It is known as the "Skeleton Coast," and humankind cannot survive there. The sea is salt water, which is not drinkable, but it brings fog to the desert, and there are many plants that are able to make use of this welcome moisture.

The shore is a frontier between two worlds. Take one step—two steps—off the sand and you're in the water. There, just a few yards from the desert, life abounds. Sea lions and otters frolic in the water, while offshore the great white shark hunts.

There are hunters in the desert.

Farther to the east lies the Kalahari Desert. It is known as a "thirstland" because there is plenty of vegetation but no permanent surface water. Hunters known as the San live there and speak a unique language full of pops and clicks. Sometimes called "Bushmen," these hunters also gather plants for food and live much as their distant ancestors did.

To put game to sleep, they coat their arrow points with a poison made from ground-up scarab beetles and plants. People in the Kalahari still need water to survive, so the San have learned how to find wild melons and juicy roots to quench their thirst. They also know how to save water from the infrequent rains in empty ostrich eggs.

The hard conditions of the desert require the San to live in small bands of tight-knit family groups. They have no leader or ruler, although the skilled hunters and older men have the most influence.

There are herds in the desert.

In the Sahel and in Ethiopia, herdsmen move with their flocks according to the rains. They live on the shore of the huge "ocean" of sand called the Sahara; in Arabic, *sahel* means "shore."

When people and livestock become too numerous at a water source, it's a catastrophe. The grazing animals eat all the plants, trample the soil, and make the water undrinkable with their wastes. The people cut down the trees and burn them for their cooking fires. The earth is thus exposed to the sun and wind, and the precious topsoil is washed away by the infrequent rains. Without soil, the land becomes sterile, and the desert grows larger.

The people and their animals must then leave in search of new water sources, repeating the cycle until each patch of land is destroyed.

There is history in the desert.

Here in the Arabian Desert, a man prays near an ancient tomb. The tombs of Arabia were sculpted by people who spent their entire lives in tents and in the open air. They thought that a "real" roof was proper only for sheltering the dead.

The desert is a place of introspection and meditation, where Moses was given the Ten Commandments, where Jesus withdrew and confronted Satan, and where Muhammad received his revelation.

It's also the place of "mirages," which fool the senses and lead travelers astray.

The desert has not always been hostile to humans. Because of the commercial routes that crossed it, great civilizations developed there: The Egyptians, the Arabs, and many others have left their traces. Timbuktu, at the gateway to the Sahara, was once a major center of culture and trade.

There is oil in the desert.

In the Arabian Desert, clouds of fire light up the night.

Today, humankind has found new riches and built new structures in the desert.

Below the desert surface are many treasures: silver, gold, copper, salt, diamonds. The most sought-after treasure is petroleum—"black gold"—which people use to make gasoline and fuel oil, as well as plastics, tires, and many other things. The modern world is utterly dependent on the use of petroleum.

Like water, petroleum is being used up far faster than the Earth could ever replace it. One day it will be completely gone, and we will need to learn to do without it.

There are holy places in the desert.

At the other end of the world, the Australian Aborigines perform a ritual dance near Ayers Rock, which they call "Uluru." This massive red rock rises straight up out of the desert and is sacred to the Aborigines.

With their bodies painted, they chant as they dance to communicate with their holy spirits. They believe in the importance of dreaming, which signifies the continuity of life. According to them, our world is born of a dream.

Like the San Bushmen, the Australian Aborigines were traditionally hunters, since Australia provided no animals suitable for herding. They killed game, such as kangaroos, with javelins and boomerangs; they fished; and they gathered plants to eat. Today there are no Aborigines who have not had some contact with modern society. They must struggle to keep their old customs alive and their holy places sacred.

There is cold in the desert.

Central Asia has huge deserts, such as the Gobi Desert, that are hot in the summer but frigid in the winter. Despite the severe change in temperature, Mongolian nomads still roam the plains and mountain slopes year round. They live in well-insulated tents, called yurts, just as they did more than 800 years ago, in the time of Genghis Khan. They are excellent horsemen, and they herd sheep, goats, cattle, and two-humped camels.

Caravans once crossed these high-altitude deserts, carrying goods along the famous route known as the "Silk Road." Ancient explorers and traders would bring precious silks from eastern Asia to the Roman Empire in the west.

Caravans carried more than goods, however; they also linked civilizations by bringing news, ideas, and religions.

There is salt in the desert.

On the other side of the globe, in Chile, the Atacama Desert is a long, desolate strip of land between the Pacific Ocean and the Andes Mountains.

It is a land of extremes, where cold and heat meet. Volcanoes smolder, and vents of scalding steam spurt and hiss.

The guanaco, a type of llama and distant cousin of the camel, wanders here, and millions of birds live on the coast. Mosses survive at the edges of salt lakes. There is a great deal of salt in these deserts because a high rate of evaporation traps salt in the soil.

The land and water sources are so salty that almost no people live here. As a result, there is practically no pollution in the Atacama, and the air is so clear that scientists have installed ultramodern telescopes on the summits to observe the stars.

There is water in the desert—a lot of water!

The frozen desert of Antarctica contains 90 percent of the world's ice (70 percent of all the freshwater on Earth!).

But the ice never melts. No plant or animal can live in the interior of the continent, because there is no liquid water there. It is the most stark and forbidding of deserts, the only one not inhabited by people—except for a few isolated scientific bases.

In contrast, the sea surrounding Antarctica teems with so much life that many animals live part of the year on, or just off, the icy shoreline. These animals include porpoises, dolphins, whales, seals, and about 45 species of birds. The most extraordinary birds are the penguins. With their wings transformed into flippers, penguins are wonderful swimmers. Emperor penguins even spend the winter in the Antarctic. They are the only warm-blooded animals (other than a few human scientists!) to stay on the continent through this coldest part of the year.

So what is the answer to our original question? Is the desert truly empty?

To Learn More:

PAGES 6–7: The Sahara is composed of *ergs* (areas of shifting sand dunes), *regs* (gravelly deserts), mountain chains, and *hammadas* (rocky plateaus). It is home to 116 species of mammals, 60 species of nesting birds, 100 species of reptiles, and around 20 species of fish. (When the pools dry up, the fish die—but their eggs lie buried in the ground and hatch when the rains come again.)

The name Sahara comes from the Arabic word *sahrá*, which means "desert," and its plural, *sahara*.

PAGES 8–9: The Tuareg nomads live in the heart of the Sahara Desert. They are found in Algeria, Mauritania, Mali, Niger, Burkina Faso, and other countries. They speak Tamashek, a Berber dialect, and their writing system is called Tifinar. The dromedary, or Arabian camel, is their inseparable companion in the desert. It is able to close its nostrils to protect itself from the sand, and can go for a long time without water thanks to its one fatty hump, which acts as a reservoir.

The old Tuareg in the illustration is squatting down to look at the S-shaped tracks left by a passing viper.

PAGES 10–11: Oases appear around a source of water, either an artesian well or a channeled *wadi* (a streambed that is usually dry except during the rainy season). Irrigation, an ancient agricultural technique that was invented in southwestern Asia, is tricky: If the water is allowed to stagnate, it evaporates; salt then concentrates in the soil and makes it sterile. The water must therefore be kept flowing, either with dams and canals or by raising water to the surface using systems of *norias* (animal- or water-powered scoop wheels). The houses in oases are usually constructed of dried mud.

PAGES 12–13: In the Mojave Desert, in southeastern California, the equivalent of many years of rainfall has been pumped from the aquifers, to supply water for thousands of private swimming pools and golf courses. Some people even use air conditioners that work by evaporation.

The Aral Sea, in central Asia, was also treated as an inexhaustible source of water and was used, among other things, to irrigate farmland in Uzbekistan, Kazakhstan, and Turkmenistan.

Its water has been disastrously reduced, and what is left is highly polluted. The fish are disappearing, and the people along the coast, who lived by fishing, are no longer able to catch enough fish to feed themselves.

PAGES 14–15: Animals of the Mojave Desert and Mexico's Sonoran Desert: The *Gila monster* on page 14 is a poisonous lizard that grows up to 2 feet long (about 60 centimeters) and feeds on small mammals, birds, and eggs.

A type of cuckoo bird, the *roadrunner* on page 15 eats insects, lizards, and snakes. Clumsy in flight, it prefers to run along the ground. At the far right of the picture is a *kangaroo rat*. This rodent's tail has a tuft at the end that helps steady it when it jumps; it can clear more than 8 feet (2½ meters) in a single leap. It gets the food and liquid it needs from seeds. The kangaroo rat in the illustration is escaping from a *rattlesnake*, a very dangerous, poisonous snake that eats small animals. It's called a rattlesnake because at the end of its tail are the hardened remains of shed skins, which produce a rattling noise when the tail moves.

Among the plants of the Mojave Desert are the *saguaro cactus*, which fills up with hundreds of gallons of water when the rains come, and the *yucca*, whose fruits and flowers were used as food by native American Indians.

PAGES 16–17: On the "Skeleton Coast," at the edge of the Namib Desert, the bones of shipwreck victims and whales are mixed with the hulks of ruined ships. Farther into the dunes, a few plants have adapted to the dryness, like the *Welwitschia*, whose huge leaves spread on the ground to catch the dew from the coastal fog. This plant can live up to 2,000 years! Animals have also adapted to the Namib Desert: The nocturnal *gecko* licks its own tears; the *scarab beetle* sips drops of fog; and the *gemsbok*, a type of antelope, has blood that is cooled before going to its brain by circulating through a fine network of capillaries under its nose.

PAGES 18–19: The climate in the Kalahari Desert becomes even drier in the winter. It's also cold, and animals and plants become scarce. The San Bushmen are forced to hunt prey such as giraffes.

The first European travelers thought the Bushmen were distinctively different in their physical features, and didn't believe that they were related to other natives of Africa. However, in modern times we realize that the San have many similarities to other African peoples.

For the Bushmen, the stars are sacred. They revere the new moon especially, its renewal symbolizing life after death. Some tribes also worship the praying mantis, thought to be the creator of the world. Others believe in two gods, one of which is the creator of the world and of living things (and of rain), and another, with lesser powers, who is partly an agent of sickness and death.

On page 18 we see a *meerkat* standing on its hind legs to warn its companions of danger. Meerkats (carnivores in the mongoose family) live in colonies of approximately thirty individuals. They eat mostly insects, scorpions, and earthworms, but also snakes, mice, birds, and birds' eggs.

PAGES 20–21: The Sahel forms a transitional zone between the arid Sahara to the north and the humid grassland to the south. The term is also applied elsewhere in Africa to describe the lands bordering the desert.

The young Ethiopian goatherd in the illustration is contributing, in spite of himself, to the desertification of the Sahel, meaning the process of turning the land into a desert through misuse. There are thousands like him who eke out a living by pasturing their small flocks on soil that will be destabilized by the loss of vegetation, allowing the relentless advance of the dunes.

However, desertification has many causes: intensive livestock raising, land clearing, wars, urbanization, massive operation of mines and oil wells, erratic changes in the climate, and off-road vehicles. According to the United Nations, the resulting damage to our environment affects nearly 8 million square miles (20 million square kilometers) of the Earth's surface.

There are a billion people on Earth who live without water that is fit for drinking!

PAGES 22–23: The tomb depicted in this illustration is located along the road to Petra, Jordan, and dates from the third century B.C.E.

Deserts have had many passionate enthusiasts like the naturalist Théodore Monod (born 1902), the missionary and explorer Charles-Eugene Foucauld (1858–1916), and writers and poets like Arthur Rimbaud (1854–91), T. E. Lawrence, better known as "Lawrence of Arabia" (1888–1935), and Antoine de Saint–Exupéry, author of *The Little Prince* (1900–44).

Did they see the mirages that the desert seems to have in such abundance? This optical illusion, which looks like a lake to many travelers, is due to the heating of the air above the sand, which makes a reversed image appear below every hill or palm tree, as if it were surrounded by water. The effect is like a mirror, hence the word *mirage*.

PAGES 24–25: Flares of burning gas rise from the chimneys of desert refineries like this one at Hassi-Messaoud, in the Algerian Sahara. Petroleum is an oil produced by the slow decomposition of aquatic plants and animals that lived hundreds of millions of years ago. It comes out of the ground as a liquid, a gas, or a solid and is currently the world's primary source of energy. It therefore brings considerable wealth to countries such as Kuwait, in the Persian Gulf, which export large amounts of this "black gold." Petroleum is a hydrocarbon, a natural mineral oil; the word comes from the Latin *petra*, "stone," and *oleum*, "oil." Deposits are found in many countries around the world.

Petroleum is found in porous rock under the ground, but also under the sea. After a deposit is located, the crude oil is brought to the surface using various drilling methods, then carried by pipelines or tanker ships to the refineries where it will be transformed into gasoline, mineral spirits, lubricating oils, fuel oil, et cetera.

A global problem caused by the burning of petroleum-derived products, like gasoline and fuel oil, is that this releases a considerable amount of carbon dioxide (CO_2) into the air. Trees and seaweed absorb 30 percent, but the surplus remains in the Earth's atmosphere and contributes to the warming of the planet.

One day we will need to find a replacement fuel and learn to better use other sources of energy, especially since the planet's reserves of petroleum could be completely exhausted in 400 years.

Elsewhere, the desert conceals other riches, including minerals (copper in Chile, diamonds in South Africa), potash, nitrates used for fertilizer, borax (used to make cleaning products), zinc, iron, uranium, and others.

PAGES 26–27: Seventy million years ago gigantic Ayers Rock, in the middle of Australia, was an island. It is over 2 miles (3.6 kilometers) long, 1,140 feet (348 meters) high, and about 5.5 miles (9 kilometers) in circumference—probably the world's largest monolith. Despite its size, it wasn't discovered by the modern world until the nineteenth century, when the first explorations into the interior of Australia began.

With those explorations came accelerated colonization and the irreversible decline of the Aborigines, who had inhabited the continent for thousands of years. Pursued by the colonists, they took refuge in the tropical forests and the deserts, but often ended up in the poor suburbs of cities and on reservations. Today they represent only 1 percent of the population of Australia.

Those who attempt to preserve a traditional way of life live by foraging and hunting—particularly kangaroos, of which there are no fewer than 47 species. The largest species, the red

kangaroo, can clear more than 30 feet (9 meters) at a bound (a record of 44 feet [13.5 meters] has been recorded) and attain a speed of 30 miles (50 kilometers) per hour. Some smaller species roam the desert all year long. The Aborigines are aided in their hunting by dingoes, wild dogs of Australia that can be tamed if they are raised from birth.

PAGES 28–29: The Gobi Desert covers about 500,000 square miles (about 1.25 million square kilometers), an area larger than Texas and California combined. Along with the Karakum, it is one of the coldest deserts in the world (as low as -22°F [-30°C] in the winter).

Yet it is home to a variety of wildlife: grouse, wolves, reindeer, sable, lynx, yaks—to say nothing of the camels. These have two humps and are called Asian camels, or Bactrian camels, from the name of an ancient country in central Asia. Besides being an invaluable means of transport for the caravan trade, camels provide the nomads with resources that are essential in the desert. Their hair is used to make tents, their hides to fashion sandals, and camel milk is consumed fresh or sour; even their dung can be used for fuel. As for their meat, some nomads eat it, but others, much like the Tuaregs of the Sahara, become so attached to their camels that they do not kill them unless the animals are injured or infirm due to old age.

PAGES 30–31: The Atacama is a cool, arid region in northern Chile. It is not well defined, but it is about 600 to 700 miles (1,000 to 1,100 kilometers) long from north to south, and is buffered from the Pacific Ocean by a line of low coastal mountains.

The desert is rich in mineral resources, including sodium nitrate and copper. They were the cause of the War of the Pacific (1879–83) in which Bolivia, Peru, and Chile struggled over access to those deposits. Chile ultimately won control of the region as a result of this war.

There is virtually no vegetation in the Atacama, but the *guanaco*, a wild llama the size of a large deer, is able to survive in this desolate land.

PAGES 32–33: Cold deserts are characterized by extreme cold and are often covered with perpetual snow or ice.

Antarctica's 5.5 million square miles (14 million square kilometers) are home to some sixty species of animals, including emperor penguins, which can stand temperatures ranging from -58°F (-50°C) to 86°F (+30°C). In fact, there are penguins that nest in hot subtropical regions, even in the Galapagos! The penguins in the illustration are not out on the Antarctic ice for the cold (the temperature never rises above freezing, even in the summer), but for the abundant fish in the sea. They live in huge colonies—which may contain up to 50,000 birds—called rookeries. Penguins do not fly but can move underwater at a speed of 30 miles (50 kilometers) per hour.

Life that depends solely on the land is limited to microscopic organisms that live in the summer, tiny wingless insects living in patches of moss and lichen, and two types of flowering plant.

SOURCES:
Encyclopaedia Britannica, Encyclopaedia Universalis, National Geographic, Quid

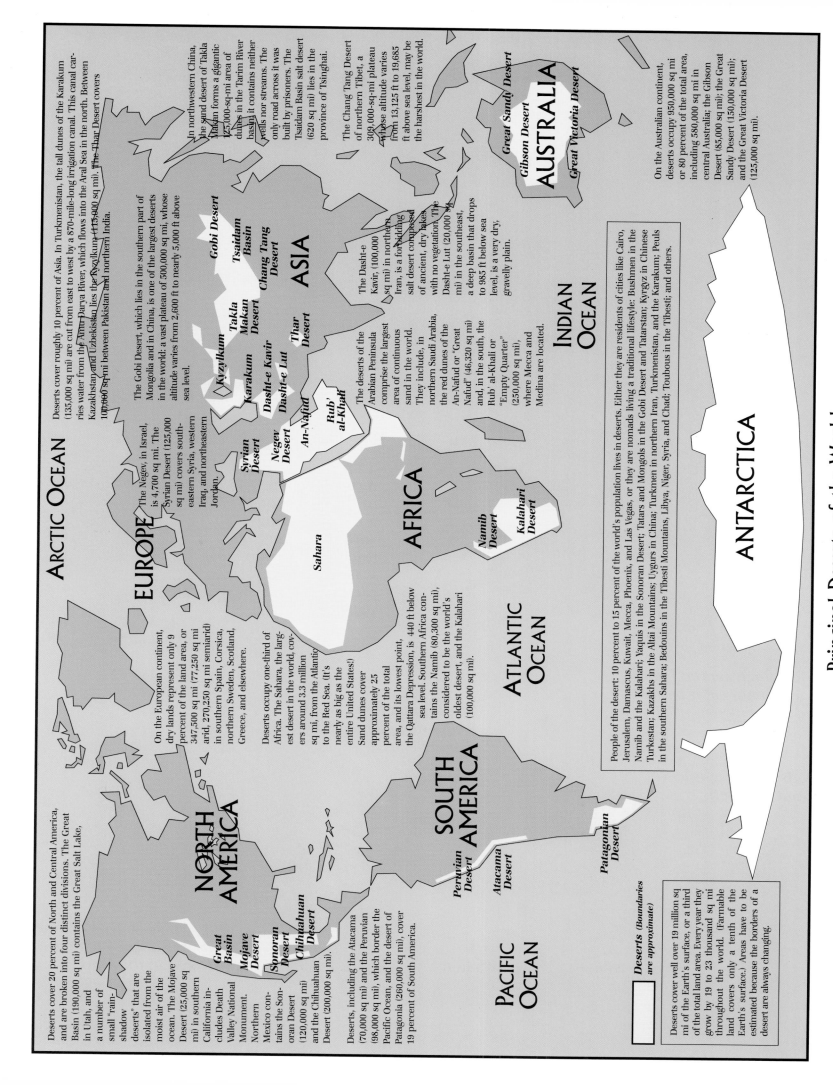

Deserts cover 20 percent of North and Central America, and are broken into four distinct divisions. The Great Basin (190,000 sq mi) in Utah, and a number of small "rain-shadow deserts" that are isolated from the moist air of the ocean. The Mojave Desert (25,000 sq mi) in southern California includes Death Valley National Monument. Northern Mexico contains the Sonoran Desert (120,000 sq mi) and the Chihuahuan Desert (200,000 sq mi).

Deserts cover roughly 10 percent of Asia. In Turkmenistan, the tall dunes of the Karakum (135,000 sq mi) are cut from east to west by a 870-mile-long irrigation canal. This canal carries water from the Amu-Darya River, which flows into the Aral Sea in the north. Between Kazakhstan and Uzbekistan lies the Kyzylkum (115,000 sq mi). The Thar Desert covers 100,000 sq mi between Pakistan and northern India.

The Gobi Desert, which lies in the southern part of Mongolia and in China, is one of the largest deserts in the world: a vast plateau of 500,000 sq mi, whose altitude varies from 2,600 ft to nearly 5,000 ft above sea level.

In northwestern China, the sand desert of 'Takla Makan forms a gigantic 125,000-sq-mi area of dunes in the Tarim River basin it contains neither wells nor streams. The only road across it was built by prisoners. The Tsaidam Basin salt desert (620 sq mi) lies in the province of Tsinghai.

The Chang Tang Desert of northern Tibet, a 309,000-sq-mi plateau whose altitude varies from 13,125 ft to 19,685 ft above sea level, may be the harshest in the world.

The Dasht-e Kavir, (100,000 sq mi in northern Iran, is a forbidding salt desert composed of ancient, dry lakes with no vegetation. The Dasht-e Lut (20,000 sq mi) in the southeast, a deep basin that drops to 985 ft below sea level, is a very dry, gravelly plain.

The deserts of the Arabian Peninsula comprise the largest area of continuous sand in the world. They include, in northern Saudi Arabia, the red dunes of the An-Nafud or "Great Nafud" (46,320 sq mi) and, in the south, the Rub' al-Khali or "Empty Quarter" (250,000 sq mi), where Mecca and Medina are located.

On the Australian continent, deserts occupy 950,000 sq mi or 80 percent of the total area, including 580,000 sq mi in central Australia; the Gibson Desert (85,000 sq mi); the Great Sandy Desert (150,000 sq mi); and the Great Victoria Desert (125,000 sq mi).

The Negev, in Israel, is 4,700 sq mi. The Syrian Desert (125,000 sq mi) covers southeastern Syria, western Iraq, and northeastern Jordan.

On the European continent, dry lands represent only 9 percent of the land area, or 347,500 sq mi (77,250 sq mi arid, 270,250 sq mi semiarid) in southern Spain, Corsica, northern Sweden, Scotland, Greece, and elsewhere.

Deserts occupy one-third of Africa. The Sahara, the largest desert in the world, covers around 3.3 million sq mi, from the Atlantic to the Red Sea. (It's nearly as big as the entire United States!) Sand dunes cover approximately 25 percent of the total area, and its lowest point, the Qattara Depression, is 440 ft below sea level. Southern Africa contains the Namib (80,300 sq mi), considered to be the world's oldest desert, and the Kalahari (100,000 sq mi).

Deserts, including the Atacama (70,000 sq mi) and the Peruvian (98,000 sq mi), which border the Pacific Ocean, and the desert of Patagonia (260,000 sq mi), cover 19 percent of South America.

People of the desert: 10 percent to 15 percent of the world's population lives in deserts. Either they are residents of cities like Cairo, Jerusalem, Damascus, Kuwait, Mecca, Phoenix, and Las Vegas, or they are nomads living a traditional lifestyle: Bushmen in the Namib and the Kalahari; Yaquis in the Sonoran Desert; Tatars and Mongols in the Gobi Desert and Tatarstan; Kyrgyz in Chinese Turkestan; Kazakhs in the Altai Mountains; Uygurs in China; Turkmen in northern Iran, Turkmenistan, and the Karakum; Peuls in the southern Sahara; Bedouins in the Tibesti Mountains, Libya, Niger, Syria, and Chad; Toubous in the Tibesti; and others.

Deserts cover well over 19 million sq mi of the Earth's surface, or a third of the total land area. Every year they grow by 19 to 23 thousand sq mi throughout the world. (Farmable land covers only a tenth of the Earth's surface.) Areas have to be estimated because the borders of a desert are always changing.

Deserts (Boundaries are approximate)

ARCTIC OCEAN · EUROPE · ASIA · AFRICA · INDIAN OCEAN · AUSTRALIA · ANTARCTICA · NORTH AMERICA · SOUTH AMERICA · PACIFIC OCEAN · ATLANTIC OCEAN

Gobi Desert · Tsaidam Basin · Chang Tang Desert · Takla Makan Desert · Kyzylkum · Karakum · Dasht-e Kavir · Dasht-e Lut · Thar Desert · An-Nafud · Rub' al-Khali · Syrian Desert · Negev Desert · Sahara · Namib Desert · Kalahari Desert · Great Sandy Desert · Gibson Desert · Great Victoria Desert · Great Basin · Mojave Desert · Sonoran Desert · Chihuahuan Desert · Peruvian Desert · Atacama Desert · Patagonian Desert

Principal Deserts of the World

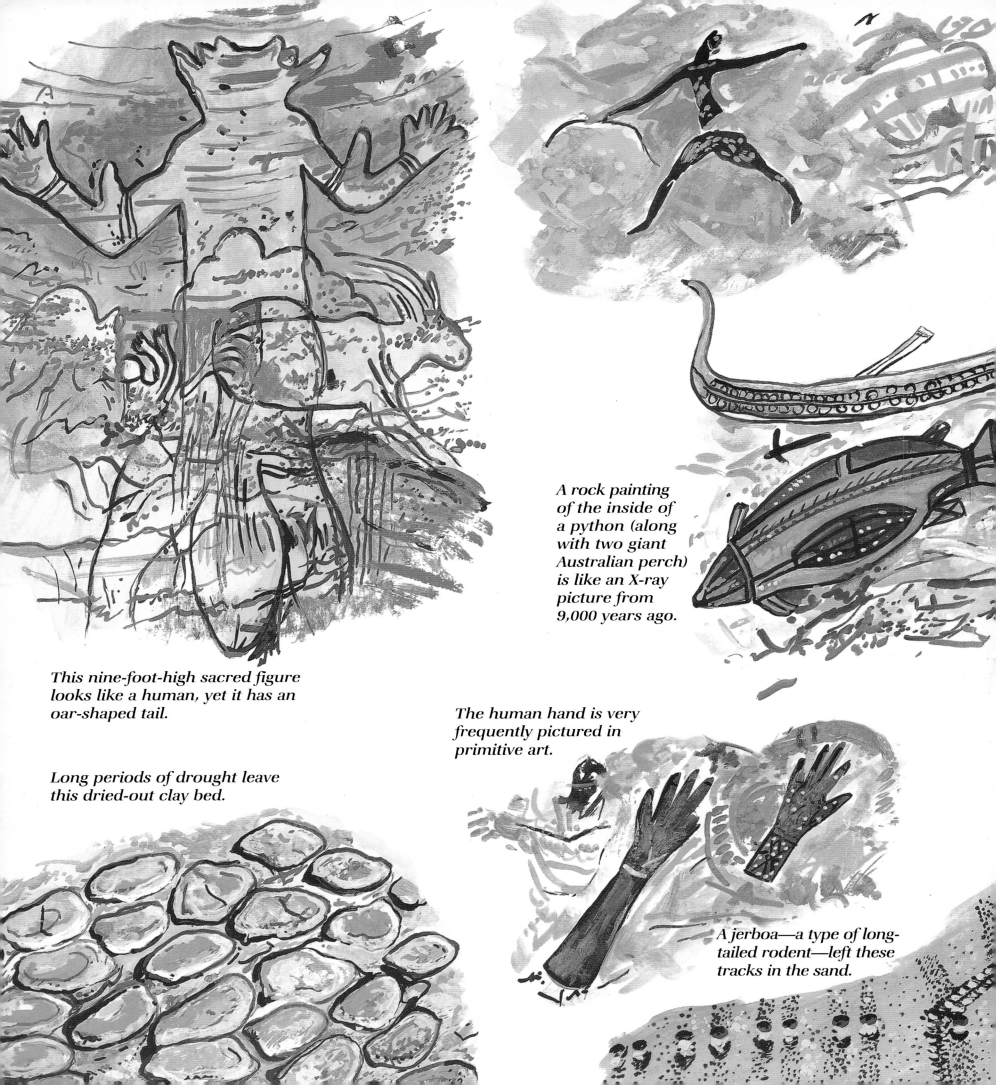

A rock painting of the inside of a python (along with two giant Australian perch) is like an X-ray picture from 9,000 years ago.

This nine-foot-high sacred figure looks like a human, yet it has an oar-shaped tail.

The human hand is very frequently pictured in primitive art.

Long periods of drought leave this dried-out clay bed.

A jerboa—a type of long-tailed rodent—left these tracks in the sand.